Arthur Miller

AUTHORED by Elizabeth Weinbloom
UPDATED AND REVISED by Adam Kissel

COVER DESIGN by Table XI Partners LLC
COVER PHOTO by Olivia Verma and © 2005 GradeSaver, LLC

BOOK DESIGN by Table XI Partners LLC

Published by GradeSaver LLC, www.gradesaver.com

First published in the United States of America by GradeSaver LLC. 2006

ISBN 978-1-60259-007-6

Printed in the United States of America

Table of Contents

Biography of Miller, Arthur (1915-2005)

Arthur Miller was one of the leading American playwrights of the twentieth century. He was born in October 1915 in New York City to a women's clothing manufacturer, who lost everything in the economic collapse of the 1930s. Living through young adulthood during the Great Depression, Miller was shaped by the poverty that surrounded him. The Depression demonstrated to the playwright the fragility and vulnerability of human existence in the modern era. After graduating from high school, Miller worked in a warehouse so that he could earn enough money to attend the University of Michigan, where he began to write plays.

Miller's first play to make it to Broadway, The Man Who Had All the Luck (1944), was a dismal failure, closing after only four performances. This early setback almost discouraged Miller from writing completely, but he gave himself one more try. Three years later, All My Sons won the New York Drama Critics' Circle Award as the best play of 1947, launching Miller into theatrical stardom. All My Sons, a drama about a manufacturer of faulty war materials, was strongly influenced by the naturalist drama of Henrik Ibsen. Along with Death of a Salesman (his most enduring success), All My Sons and The Man Who Had All the Luck form a thematic trilogy of plays about love triangles involving fathers and sons. The drama of the family is at the core of all of Miller's major plays, but nowhere is it more prominent than in the realism of All My Sons and the impressionism of Death of a Salesman.

Death of a Salesman (1949) secured Miller's reputation as one of the nation's foremost playwrights. Death of a Salesman mixes the tradition of social realism that informs most of Miller's work with a more experimental structure that includes fluid leaps in time as the protagonist, Willy Loman, drifts into memories of his sons as teenagers. Loman represents an American archetype, a victim of his own delusions of grandeur and obsession with success, which haunt him with a sense of failure.

Miller won a Tony Award for Death of a Salesman as well as a Pulitzer Prize. The play has been frequently revived in film, television, and stage versions that have included actors such as Dustin Hoffman, George C. Scott and, most recently, Brian Dennehy in the part of Willy Loman.

Miller followed Death of a Salesman with his most politically significant work, The Crucible (1953), a tale of the Salem witch trials that contains obvious analogies to the McCarthy anti-Communist hearings in 1950s America. The highly controversial nature of the politics of The Crucible, which lauds those who refuse to name names, led to the play's mixed response. In later years, however, it has become one of the most studied and performed plays of American theater.

Three years after The Crucible, in 1956, Miller found himself persecuted by the very force that he warned against, when he was called to testify before the House Un-American Activities Committee. Miller refused to name people he allegedly saw at a Communist writers' meeting a decade before, and he was convicted of contempt. He later won an appeal.

Also in 1956, Miller married actress Marilyn Monroe. The two divorced in 1961, one year before her death. That year Monroe appeared in her last film, The Misfits, which is based on an original screenplay by Miller. After divorcing Monroe, Miller wed Ingeborg Morath, to whom he remained married until his death in 2005. The pair had a son and a daughter.

Miller also wrote the plays A Memory of Two Mondays and the short A View from the Bridge, which were both staged in 1955. His other works include After the Fall (1964), a thinly veiled account of his marriage to Monroe, as well as The Price (1967), The Archbishop's Ceiling (1977), and The American Clock (1980). His most recent works include the plays The Ride Down Mt. Morgan (1991), The Last Yankee (1993), and Broken Glass (1993), which won the Olivier Award for Best Play.

Although Miller did not write frequently for film, he did pen an adaptation for the 1996 film version of The Crucible starring Daniel Day-Lewis and Winona Ryder, which garnered him an Academy Award nomination. Miller's daughter Rebecca married Day-Lewis in 1996.

About All My Sons

When the young playwright Arthur Miller began writing All My Sons, he was embarking on a project that would be either the beginning or the end of his career. His first and only play to be produced on Broadway, *The Man Who Had All the Luck*, was an unmitigated failure, lasting only four performances. A practical man who had lived through the depression, Miller decided to give himself one more chance. If he did not have success with his next play, then he would quit the business and find "another line of work."

In the meantime, Tennessee Williams had met great success with The Glass Menagerie in 1945, a very personal and psychological play with poetic overtones. Miller's plays, on the other hand, are public works, with straightforward (though not unpoetic) language, and which address issues of the individual's public persona and how people act. But he learned from Williams's success and set out to write a more commercial play, a drama that would "land" with audiences, in the language of the Broadway business. He also chose to write a play in a realistic style, a problem play in the manner of Henrik Ibsen, evoking a style he had not used in many years. The work of Ibsen influenced All My Sons structurally as well, for Ibsen had liberally applied the principle of Greek theater that stresses the influence of the past on the present.

When the play was finished after five years of work, Miller asked his agent to send it to the director Elia Kazan. A former member of the Communist Party, Kazan had directed Williams's The Glass Menagerie, and he would later direct the genre-redefining A Streetcar Named Desire and Death of a Salesman (and would win Academy Awards for *Gentleman's Agreement* and *On the Waterfront*). Kazan's career was tarnished in memory, however, and his relationship with Miller was permanently severed when he chose to name names for the House Un-American Activities Commission during the Red Scare. But at the time, as a successful director with a talent for eliciting monumental performances from his actors, and as someone who shared Miller's leftist politics, Kazan was the perfect choice for All My Sons. The cast included such rising stars as Ed Begley (as Keller, later of Inherit the Wind), Arthur Kennedy (as Chris, later creator of the roles of Biff Loman and John Proctor), and Karl Malden (as George, later of *Streetcar*, *Tea and Sympathy*, and *On The Waterfront*).

Luckily for Miller and for the American stage, All My Sons was a success. Opening at the Coronet Theatre on January 29, 1947, the first night's notices were mixed--with the crucial exception of the *New York Times*, whose Brooks Atkinson admired Miller as a genuine new talent. As usual, the *Times* review swayed all the others, and All My Sons ran for 328 performances (quite respectable at that time) and won the New York Drama Critics' Circle award for best play of 1947, beating out Eugene O'Neill's *The Iceman Cometh* (which at the time had been coolly received and would only become a landmark of American drama in retrospect).

Miller's success gave him financial stability, confidence, and the confirmation of Miller's identity as a playwright. This success was necessary for him to take a risk with his next work, Death of a Salesman.

Character List

Joe Keller

Middle aged and prosperous, Joe Keller is a family man whose world does not extend beyond the borders of his front yard or the gate around his factory. He is not a greedy, conniving caricature of capitalism, but rather a good-natured and loving man of little education, whose myopic perspective on his world stems from a devotion to his family and an education in a society that encourages generally antisocial behavior. American rugged individualism alienated Keller, whose past misdeeds haunt the future of his family.

Kate Keller (Mother)

Though she has a successful husband and a loving son, Mother cannot abandon the memory of her other son, who was lost in the war. Her delusions about Larry's disappearance and her vehement self-denial are symptomatic of greater issues than just a grief-stricken mother's inability to cope with the loss of a child. Nervous and suspicious, Mother has taken on the burden of her husband's secret while he presents the face of an untroubled conscience to the world, while she suffers from headaches and nightmares. Her fantasies about Larry are constructed from a sense of self-preservation, and the flimsy basis for her hopes is threatened any time someone who loved Larry intimates that he or she may not share Kate's confidence in his return.

Chris Keller

Returning from the war as a hero, Chris found the day-to-day provincialism of his old life stifling. But Chris is a family man, and he is devoted to his parents. He is uncomfortable with the success his father's business found during the war, when so many of his comrades died pointlessly. He redirects his discomfort into an idealism and an attitude of social awareness that is foreign to his family environment. Others perceive Chris's idealism as oppressive, asking sacrifices of others that Chris himself does not make as he lives comfortably (if guiltily) on his father's dime.

Larry Keller

Although he has been dead for some years by the start of the play, Larry is as much a character in the play as anyone who actually appears on stage. His disappearance haunts his family through his mother's superstitious belief in his return, as well as through his brother's wary but measured rejection of Larry's claim on his childhood sweetheart. Larry is constantly compared to Chris throughout the play, ostensibly for the purpose of better defining the character of Chris, but in the end we learn that Larry's own character had quite an effect on the story. Larry is portrayed by his father as the more sensible and practical of his sons, the one with a head for business who would understand his father's arguments. Larry, not Chris, possessed the stronger sense of honor and connectedness, and Larry sacrificed himself in penance for his father's misdeeds.

Ann Deever

The beautiful Ann has not become attached to a new man since her beau Larry died in the war, but this is not through lack of suitors. Ann is mired in the past, though she has not been waiting for Larry to return. Rather, she has waited for his brother Chris to step forward and take Larry's place in her heart. She is an honest, down-to-earth girl, and she is emboldened by the strength of certain of her convictions. Sharing Chris's idealism and righteousness, she has shunned her father for his crimes during the war, and she fully understands his assertion that if he had any suspicions of his own father, he could not live with himself. Ann and her brother work to establish "appropriate" reactions to a father's wartime racketeering.

George Deever

George serves a mostly functional role in the story of the Keller family. His arrival in the second act is a catalyst for a situation that was on edge from long-established tensions. His disdain is for the crime, not for the man, and now that he has been newly convinced of his father's innocence, he is here to rescue his sister from entering the family of the man he believes is actually guilty. Yet George is easily disarmed by Keller's good humor, and his own convictions about his father's innocence are almost undermined by his awareness of his father's other faults and weaknesses.

Dr. Jim Bayliss

The neighborhood doctor, Jim is a good man who believes in the duty of one man to help another, but he at the same time acknowledges a man's responsibility to his family. He is interested in medicine not for the money but to help people. This point is dramatized by his reluctance to bother with a hypochondriac. He once left his wife to do medical research, but he eventually went home, putting his responsibility to his family ahead of his responsibility to the world.

Sue Bayliss

Jim's wife Sue put her husband through medical school, and she expects more than gratitude in return. She blames Chris's infectious, insinuating idealism for her husband's interest in the fiscally unrewarding field of medical research.

Frank Lubey

A simple neighbor, Frank has an interest in astrology. Mother asked him before the start of the play to prepare a horoscope for Larry in order to determine his "favorable day."

Lydia Lubey

Now married to Frank, Lydia is a former sweetheart of George's, but she did not wait for him to return from the war. Seeing Lydia makes George wistful about the simpler life he could have had, if he had not left home for the greater world of New York.

Bert

Bert is a neighborhood boy who plays cop-and-robber games with Joe Keller, to Mother's chagrin. Keller has allowed Bert and the other children to get the story of his jail time wrong and to believe that he is a chief of police with a jail in his basement. Mother is made very anxious by these games.

Major Themes

Relatedness

Arthur Miller stated that the issue of relatedness is the main one in *All My Sons*. The play introduces questions that involve an individual's obligation to society, personal responsibility, and the distinction between private and public matters. Keller can live with his actions during the war because he sees himself as answerable only to himself and his family, not to society as a whole. Miller criticizes Keller's myopic worldview, which allows him to discount his crimes because they were done "for the family." The principal contention is that Keller is wrong in his claim that there is nothing greater than the family, since there is a whole world to which Keller is connected. To cut yourself off from your relationships with society at large is to invite tragedy of a nature both public (regarding the pilots) and private (regarding the suicides).

The Nuclear Family

The reverse side of Miller's relatedness argument is his downplaying of the family as the nucleus of society. Somehow people are to feel a more general caring for others that is not drawn off by family obligations. What, then, is the place of the family in the larger social system? Discussions of the family serve mostly to contrast characters' opinions about an individual's responsibilities to the family versus society at large. The family is also presented as a unit that can be corrupted and damaged by the actions and denials of its individuals, a small-scale example of the way individual actions can corrupt society.

The Past

All My Sons is a play about the past. It is inescapable--but how exactly does it affect the present and shape the future? Can crimes ever be ignored or forgotten? Most of the dialogue involves various characters discovering various secrets about the recent history of the Keller family. Miller shows how these past secrets have affected those who have kept them. The revelation of the secrets is presented as unavoidable--they were going to come out at some point, no matter what, and it is through Miller's manipulation of the catalysts that the truths are all revealed on the same day. Whilte the revelations are unavoidable, so are their fatal consequences.

Denial and Self-Deception

How do we deceive ourselves and others? We select things to focus on in life, but do we also need to deny certain things in order to live well? What toll does denial take on the psyche, the family, and society? Two main facts about the Keller family history must be confronted. One is Larry's death, and the other is Keller's responsibility for the shipment of defective parts. Mother denies the first while accepting the second, and Keller accepts the first while denying the second. The result is that both characters live in a state of self-deception, willfully ignoring one of the truths so that the family can continue to function in acceptable ways.

Idealism

Chris is described by other characters as an idealist, although we do not see this trait in action aside from his angry response to the wartime profiteering. Yet the others define him by his idealism, setting him apart as a man of scruples. Chris decides that he must abandon these scruples to the cause of practicality when he is faced with the prospect of sending his father to jail. Is idealism sustainable in a fallen, complex world? If ideals must be sacrificed, is there any supervening ideal or principle to help us decide which ideals should be sacrificed in which circumstances?

Business

Keller argues that his actions during the war were defensible ass requirements of good business practice. He also frequently defines himself as an uneducated man, taking pride in his commercial success without traditional book learning. Yet, his sound business sense actually leads to his downfall. This failure is connected with Miller's leftist politics and the play's overall criticisms (shared by some conservatives) of a capitalist system that encourages individuals to value their business sense over their moral sense. How could rules that govern business be exempt from the moral norms and laws governing the rest of society?

Blame

Each character in the play has a different experience of blame. Joe Keller tries to blame anyone and everyone for crimes during the war, first by letting his partner go to jail. Later, when he is confronted with the truth, he blames business practice and the U.S. Army and everyone he can think of--except himself. When he finally does accept blame, after learning how Larry had taken the blame and shame on himself, Keller kills himself. Chris, meanwhile, feels guilty for surviving the war and for having money, but when the crimes are revealed, he places the blame squarely on his father's shoulders. He even blames his father for his own inability to send his father to prison. These are just a few examples of the many instances of deflected blame in this story, and this very human impulse is used to great effect by Miller to demonstrate the true relationships and power plays between characters as they try to maintain self-respect as well as personal and family honor.

The American Dream

Miller points out the flaw with a merely economic interpretation of the American Dream as business success alone. Keller sacrifices other parts of the American Dream for simple economic success. Has he given up part of his basic human decency (consider the pilots) and a successful family life--does he sacrifice Steve or Larry? Miller suggests the flaws of a capitalist who has no grounding in cultural or social morals. While Keller accepted the idea that a good businessman like himself should patch over the flawed shipment, Miller critiques a system that would encourage profit and greed at the expense of human life and happiness. The challenge is to recover the full American Dream of healthy communities with thriving families, whether or not capitalism is the economic system that leads to this happy life. Economic mobility alone can be detrimental--consider George's abandonment of his hometown for big city success. There is a rift in the Bayliss marriage over Dr. Bayliss's desire to do unprofitable research, because his wife wants him to make more money instead of do what he enjoys and what will help others.

Glossary of Terms

ambiguous
doubtful, open to multiple interpretations

cockpit
the space in an airplane where the pilot controls the craft

dast
dare not

exasperated
angry, impatient, annoyed

foreman
man who serves as the leader of a crew of workers

haberdasher
person who sells men's clothes

horoscope
astrological forecast of a person's future, determined by analyzing the configuration of the planets and stars on any particular day in relation to their configuration on the person's birthday

idealism
a vision and pursuit of the best possible world, believing it to be achievable

ignoramus
an ignorant person

liable
responsible; likely

mum's the word
an idiomatic expression for "say nothing about it"

P-40
a single-occupancy aircraft flown in World War II

parole

release of a prisoner during the sentence, on condition of good conduct

peevish
ill-tempered, cranky

penitentiary
jail

solicitude
care or concern for the well-being of another

trellis
archway of latticework on which plants often are grown

unabashed
not embarrassed, poised

yellow
cowardly

Zeppelin
an airship, like a blimp

Short Summary

Joe and Kate Keller had two sons, Chris and Larry. Keller owned a manufacturing plant with Steve Deever, and their families were close. Steve's daughter Ann was Larry's beau, and George was their friend. When the war came, both Keller boys and George were drafted.

During the war, Keller's and Deever's manufacturing plant had a very profitable contract with the U.S. Army, supplying airplane parts. One morning, a shipment of defective parts came in. Under pressure from the army to keep up the output, Steve Deever called Keller, who had not yet come into work that morning, to ask what he should do. Keller told Steve to weld the cracks in the airplane parts and ship them out. Steve was nervous about doing this alone, but Keller said that he had the flu and could not go into work. Steve shipped out the defective but possibly safe parts on his own.

Later, it was discovered that the defective parts caused twenty-one planes to crash and their pilots to die. Steve and Keller were arrested and convicted, but Keller managed to win an appeal and get his conviction overturned. He claimed that Steve did not call him and that he was completely unaware of the shipment. Keller went home free, while Steve remained in jail, shunned by his family.

Meanwhile, overseas, Larry received word about the first conviction. Racked with shame and grief, he wrote a letter to Ann telling her that she must not wait for him. Larry then went out to fly a mission, during which he broke out of formation and crashed his plane, killing himself. Larry was reported missing.

Three years later, the action of the play begins. Chris has invited Ann to the Keller house because he intends to propose to her--they have renewed their contact in the last few years while she has been living in New York. They must be careful, however, since Mother insists that Larry is still alive somewhere. Her belief is reinforced by the fact that Larry's memorial tree blew down in a storm that morning, which she sees as a positive sign. Her superstition has also led her to ask the neighbor to make a horoscope for Larry in order to determine whether the day he disappeared was an astrologically favorable day. Everyone else has accepted that Larry is not coming home, and Chris and Keller argue that Mother should learn to forget her other son. Mother demands that Keller in particular should believe that Larry is alive, because if he is not, then their son's blood is on Keller's hands.

Ann's brother George arrives to stop the wedding. He had gone to visit Steve in jail to tell him that his daughter was getting married, and then he left newly convinced that his father was innocent. He accuses Keller, who disarms George by being friendly and confident. George is reassured until Mother accidentally says that Keller has not been sick in fifteen years. Keller tries to cover her slip of the tongue by adding the exception of his flu during the war, but it is now too late. George is again convinced of Keller's guilt, but Chris tells him to leave the house.

Chris's confidence in his father's innocence is shaken, however, and in a confrontation with his parents, he is told by Mother that he must believe that Larry is alive. If Larry is dead, Mother claims, then it means that Keller killed him by shipping out those defective parts. Chris shouts angrily at his father, accusing him of being inhuman and a murderer, and he wonders aloud what he must do in response to this unpleasant new information about his family history.

Chris is disillusioned and devastated, and he runs off to be angry at his father in privacy. Mother tells Keller that he ought to volunteer to go to jail--if Chris wants him to. She also talks to Ann and continues insisting that Larry is alive. Ann is forced to show Mother the letter that Larry wrote to her before he died, which was essentially a suicide note. The note basically confirms Mother's belief that if Larry is dead, then Keller is responsible--not because Larry's plane had the defective parts, but because Larry killed himself in response to the family responsibility and shame due to the defective parts.

Mother begs Ann not to show the letter to her husband and son, but Ann does not comply. Chris returns and says that he is not going to send his father to jail, because that would accomplish nothing and his family practicality has finally overcome his idealism. He also says that he is going to leave and that Ann will not be going with him, because he fears that she will forever wordlessly ask him to turn his father in to the authorities.

Keller enters, and Mother is unable to prevent Chris from reading Larry's letter aloud. Keller now finally understands that in the eyes of Larry and in a symbolic moral sense, all the dead pilots were his sons. He says that he is going into the house to get a jacket, and then he will drive to the jail and turn himself in. But a moment later, a gunshot is heard--Keller has killed himself.

Summary and Analysis of Act I

All My Sons takes place in a small American town in August, a few years after World War II. The events of the play occur on a single set, the back yard of the Keller home, where a tree has recently been torn down by a storm. The Kellers are solidly middle-class and have a working-class background. They are not rich, but they are financially comfortable, and there is a sense throughout the play that they worked hard to reach this state of stability.

At curtain rise, Joe Keller and Dr. Jim Bayliss are in the yard. Keller is a middle-aged father, uneducated but sensible and generally unexceptional. Jim, the local doctor, is making small talk with his neighbor. After some talk about the weather, another neighbor enters. Frank Lubey is younger, pleasant, and profoundly superstitious.

Keller is reading the want ads in the Sunday paper, and he is quietly impressed by all the different types of business there are nowadays. Frank notices the broken tree, and Keller replies sadly that it fell the previous night. His wife has not yet seen it. Frank refers obliquely to the fact that the tree was planted in memory of Keller's son Larry, who would have turned 27 this month. Frank knows Larry's birthday because he has been preparing a horoscope for Larry at the request of Keller's wife Kate (referred to in the stage directions as "Mother" throughout). She wishes to know if November 25th, the day on which Larry went missing in the war, was a favorable day for her son. According to those who believe in these things (that is, Frank and Kate, but not Keller), it would have been fairly impossible for Larry to die on a favorable day.

Keller mentions that a girl named Annie is upstairs sleeping, and the mention of her makes Jim and Frank excited. Jim is new to the neighborhood, so he has never met Annie, and Frank is eager to see an old acquaintance. Sue Bayliss, Jim's wife, stops by to tell Jim that a patient is on the phone. Jim implies that the patient in question is a hypochondriac, and Sue suggests that he should be happy to take his doctor's fee whether the patient is really sick or not. Sue mentions that Annie should stop by later to see what they have done to the house she used to live in, and they exit.

Lydia Lubey, Frank's wife, enters to complain of a broken toaster, and then Frank exits. Lydia lingers for a moment to ask if Annie is still unmarried (she is). Lydia finds that hard to believe, and Keller replies bitterly that it is because of the war that Annie is single and that he has one son instead of two. She exits.

Chris Keller enters. He is an affectionate young man of 32, who clearly adores his father. They wonder what Mother will say about the broken tree. A little boy named Bert runs in. He and Keller have an extended make-believe game in which Keller is the police inspector and Bert has been deputized to arrest other children in the town. After being told that there is a jail in the basement of the house, Bert leaves to continue his patrol.

Chris and Keller resume conversation about the tree. Early that morning, during the storm, Chris saw his mother standing outside beside the tree when it cracked. She had been crying very hard and wandering around at night, like she did shortly after Larry died. Although Larry has been missing for several years, Mother still thinks that he is alive somewhere. Chris thinks it is dishonest that he and Keller allow her to hold onto this dream, while they themselves are rather certain that Larry is long dead. Keller is resistant to making this fact final, however, because they cannot prove that their son is dead, at least not to his wife, without a body or a grave.

Chris sits him down and says that he asked Annie to visit because he is going to propose to her. Keller is lukewarm about the idea, because Annie was Larry's girl. From Mother's perspective, Larry is not dead, so Annie is not available to Chris. But Chris insists that there is no other girl for him, even though they have not seen each other since the war. He declares an ultimatum: if his parents will not accept his marriage to Annie, then he and Annie will just get married and move elsewhere. Keller is shocked that Chris would leave behind the family business.

Mother appears. She is somewhat younger than her husband, and she is very loving. She says that it is funny that Larry's tree blew down in his birthday month, and this shows that he is coming back. Uncomfortable, Chris tries to change the subject and talk about how good Annie looks. Mother says that she loves Annie because she did not run off with another man as soon as her beau was declared missing. Mother has a headache, perhaps from a bad dream in which she saw Larry reaching to her from the cockpit of his plane. She sees this as more evidence that they had been hasty in putting a memorial tree up for him.

Chris says that maybe they should be trying to forget Larry, and Mother is furious. Chris exits to get her some aspirin, and Mother asks Keller if Chris intends to propose to Annie. He answers noncommittally. Mother says that if Annie is still single, that means that she has been waiting for Larry, and they dare not take her faith away. Mother gets somewhat hysterical, claiming that if Larry is not coming back, then she will kill herself. She says that Keller in particular should still believe--but Keller does not understand why he in particular should believe. Bert reappears, but Mother shoos him away, saying that they must end that jail business.

Ann and Chris enter. She is beautiful and strong-willed. Their entrance cuts short the argument. Jim and Sue briefly enter and are introduced to Ann. Before she leaves, Sue tells Ann that she should never, not even in her mind, count her husband's money. Ann and the Kellers discuss their plans for the evening, and Mother mentions that the room Ann is staying in was Larry's room. She is shocked, because the closet is full of clothes and the shoes are shined. There is an awkward moment, and Mother pulls Ann aside to gossip. Ann says that her parents are not getting divorced. Mother asks if Ann goes out much, and Ann knows that she is really asking if she is still waiting for Larry. She says that she is not. Mother insists that deep in her heart she must think he is still alive. Ann asks why Mother still believes, and Mother says it is because "certain things can never be," not in a world with a God.

Frank enters and asks Ann about her brother George, the lawyer. He also asks when her father expects parole, and Ann clams up. After Frank leaves, she is dismayed to realize that the town is still talking about her father, even though he has been gone and in prison for years now. Keller claims that no one talks about the case any more, because when he got out of prison he walked down the street with his head held high. It is slowly established that Keller and Ann's father Steve had been in business together during the war, and they had sold a shipment of cracked cylinder heads to the Air Force, which made twenty-one P-40s crash. The two were tried, and Steve was found guilty and sent to jail, but Keller went home. Ann is surprised that Keller does not hold any grudges against her father, even though her father had tried to blame the whole thing on him. Ann does hold a grudge, though; she has not spoken to her father since then. Chris agrees and calls Steve a murderer. For all they know, Ann says, one of those cracked cylinder heads could have been in the plane that crashed with Larry inside. Mother is angered by this remark, and she insists that it all has nothing to do with Larry. Keller says that Steve was a little man who followed orders when the army called for the cylinder heads, and that the incident was just a mistake, not murder.

The parents exit, and Ann says that she will not stay. Chris changes her mind by confessing his love. But their embrace is unsatisfactory to Ann, and Chris explains that he feels uncomfortable in his happiness because he survived the war, while all the other men in his company did not. Ann says that Chris should be happy with his good fortune and proud of his money and his business.

Keller enters and says that George, Ann's brother, is on the phone. Ann exits to answer the phone. Keller expresses puzzlement that George is calling from Columbus, where his father's prison is. Keller is suspicious that George and Ann are trying to open up the case again, and Chris is angered by the insinuation. Keller changes the subject and says he wants to rename the business for Chris, but Chris is uneasy with the proposition. Keller suspects that Chris is ashamed of their money, and he insists that it is good money, moral money. Ann returns and says that George will be coming that night. She and Chris leave. Mother enters and is shaken by the fact that George needs to speak to Ann. She asks what it is Steve has to tell George that has required George to take an airplane from New York to see him. Keller insists there is nothing, and Mother twice questions his resolve on that matter. Mother finishes with a warning that Keller ought to be smart.

Analysis

The important events in All My Sons have already transpired. The only action that occurs within the time frame of the narrative is the revelation of certain facts about the past, and it is important to track how the revelations change the relationships among the characters as well as their own self-definition. Arthur Miller carefully controls the flow of information rather than focusing on plot and action. Thus the play, influenced by the work of the playwright Ibsen, is paced by the slow revelation of facts. In the first act, not much is said that is unknown to the characters, but it is all new to the audience. Miller takes his time revealing the background information to the audience by having the characters obliquely refer to Larry and to his disappearance again and again, until all the necessary information has been revealed through natural dialog. The explanation of Keller's and Steve's business during the war, and the ensuing scandal, is similarly revealed through insinuation and association. The first reference to Steve's incarceration occurs when Ann says that her mother and father will probably live together again "when he gets out." This does not mean much to the audience until Frank asks about Steve's parole. Therefore, Ann's estrangement from her father and the community's hostility and curiosity towards the man are established before the audience knows exactly where Steve is and how he got there. Miller's manipulation of the background information heightens the anticipation and the curiosity of the audience.

Again, very little new information is presented to the characters in this act. Chris reveals his intentions to marry Ann to his father, Ann learns of Chris's feelings of guilt for surviving the war and coming home to a successful business, and Mother learns that Ann has not exactly been waiting for Larry all these years. Yet Miller's skillful and carefully planned withholding of the characters' backgrounds prevents the first act from feeling like forty minutes of exposition--which, in function, it actually is. The slow pace of the first act also allows the horror of the crime to seep into the atmosphere, imbuing the audience with a sense that this idyllic, placid community has been injected with a slow poison.

In addition, as in many plays and written works, Miller's choices in establishing the relationships in this fashion allow him to closely manipulate the audience's inferences and judgments about each character. (The effect is not unlike that of F. Scott Fitzgerald's The Great Gatsby, in which the first-person narrator, speaking after the events of the narrative, slowly reveals Daisy Buchanan's character to the reader.) Yet Arthur Miller did not have the narrative tools of the novel at his disposal like Fitzgerald did. A playwright mainly employs dialogue. Therefore, readers and viewers should pay careful attention to the ways that Miller sets up the necessary details about each character and their relationships. Keller's insistence that Steve was not a murderer, and Chris's strong belief that patching those cracked airplane heads was morally reprehensible, are not just foreshadowing. They are essential elements of each character's personal trajectory, and these elements express the principal concept of the play: the past has an enduring influence on the present which never quite goes away. Fitzgerald's work leaves the reader with the message that one "can't repeat the past," and Miller's adds the caveat that one cannot ignore the past either.

The first act also illustrates the tensions between the characters that will rise to the surface in the second and third acts. The Kellers seem like a happy family at first; it is even remarked that Chris is the rare sort of person who truly loves his parents. But there is resentment beneath the surface of their contented existence, resentment that reflects more than just grief at the loss of a son. Larry was clearly the favored of the Keller boys. Keller compares Larry's business sense to Chris's lack of it, and Chris complains that he has always played second fiddle to Larry in the eyes of his parents and of Ann, who was first betrothed to Larry. The family sometimes implies bitterness that Chris, not Larry, was the son who survived the war. Chris is too idealistic, too soft about business. Like Michael Corleone in Mario Puzo's *The Godfather*, Chris returned from the war with a new idealism that will not permit him to condone his father's shadier business practices. And like Vito Corleone, Keller believes that his actions are legitimate if he acts for the sake of his family. In the end, like Michael Corleone, Chris must compromise his values in order to protect his father and his own family.

Mother's insecurities are expressed through her obsessive delusions about her dead son. She is anxious, suspicious of Ann, and highly superstitious. She cannot handle her husband's casual "jail" game with the neighborhood children, because there is something weighing on her conscience. Jail has been a real specter in this family. When Keller responds to her worries with "what have I got to hide?" we see the first clue that he does have something to hide after all--and Mother knows all about it--and it makes her sick with worry.

Ann is more of a simple character, serving the purpose of the plot but not actually a focus of the plot herself. All My Sons is the story of the Kellers, so we do not see much of Ann's reaction to the realization that her father was largely innocent after all. She functions in this act as a catalyst, a femme fatale in the literal sense, the woman who brings destruction to the false calm of the Kellers' life by churning up a past that some of the family, in some ways, has tried to ignore. She and George have their own family drama, but Miller keeps a tight focus, so Ann's and George's story is not the subject of this play except inasmuch as their disgust for their father heightens the tension between another son and a father who might be guilty.

Summary and Analysis of Act II

The second act takes place later the same day. Mother tells Chris that she fears that George is coming to open up the case again. Mother leaves, and Ann tells Chris that they ought to tell her about the engagement soon. Chris leaves, and Ann gossips with the neighbor Sue for awhile. Sue complains that her husband resents her for having put him through medical school, saying that "you can never owe somebody without resenting them." Sue says that Jim wants to do medical research and that Chris is the one who put idealistic thoughts of helping the world into her husband's head. She thinks that Chris makes other men feel guilty about their lives, while Chris lives on his father's business--she implies that this is not clean money.

Chris enters, and Sue speaks cordially to him, then leaves. Ann tells Chris that Sue hates him and says that everyone thinks Keller is guilty. Chris says that there is no suspicion in his mind whatsoever, asking if she thought he could possibly forgive his father if he had been guilty. Keller enters, and they lightheartedly banter about his lack of education. Keller says that everybody is getting so educated that there will be no one left to take away the garbage. "It's gettin' so the only dumb ones left are the bosses ... you stand on the street today and spit, you're gonna hit a college man." Keller changes the subject and offers to give Ann's father a job when he gets out of jail, ostensibly so that he will not freeload on the newlyweds. Keller takes it as a personal insult when Ann implies that she would never have anything to do with Steve, father or not. Keller leaves.

Jim announces that George is about to enter, and he warns Chris that George has blood in his eye--he should not fight this out in front of his mother. George enters, and there is some cordial but strained small talk for awhile. Eventually, George cuts to the chase and tells Ann that she is not going to marry Chris, because his father ruined her family. George explains that he went to the jail to tell their father that Ann was getting married, and he discovered that they had been wrong all along. They did a terrible thing in cutting their father out of their lives. Steve had been alone at work when the cracked cylinder heads came in, so he called Keller. Keller told him to weld the cracks and send the parts on to the army, but Steve was afraid to do it alone. Keller claimed that he had the flu and could not go into work. This excuse made it possible for him later to deny any involvement in the shipment. Chris says he heard all this before in court, but George says it was different hearing it directly from his father, a "frightened mouse" of a man who would never do such a thing on his own volition. Chris counters that he certainly would, and because he was such a frightened mouse he would throw the blame on someone else because he was not man enough to take the heat. George accuses Chris, saying that he must know the family secret, and that this is why his name is not on the business. Chris warns him not to start a fight.

Mother enters; there is a general pause. She gushes over George for a while, and he responds kindly, since they have always gotten along. Lydia stops by (she and

George were old sweethearts), and it saddens him to see her. Everyone is happy and friendly until Keller enters. George says that his father is not doing well, and Keller is sympathetic. George tries to be hostile, but he keeps getting disarmed by Keller's friendliness. Keller says he is sad to hear that Steve is still angry at him and that Steve never knew how to take the blame. He rattles off a list of incidents in which Steve tried to blame others to save face. George knows that this is true, and his anger is diffused. He decides to stay for dinner after all, and he comments that everything looks the same and everyone looks well.

Mother responds proudly that her husband has not been sick for fifteen years. Keller hastily adds the exception of his flu during the war. Mother takes a moment before she realizes what he is talking about, and George notices the awkwardness. His suspicion is reawakened.

Frank enters and announces that he has finished Larry's horoscope. The day he disappeared was his favorable day, so Larry probably could not have been killed on that day. Mother insists that Larry is alive, and she says that she has packed Ann's bag and it is time for her to go. George keeps insisting on returning to Mother's slip-up on the matter of Keller's flu during the war, and George tries to get Ann to leave with him. She says she will not leave till Chris tells her to, and Chris throws George out. Ann runs after him, after all, to try to calm him down.

The Kellers are left alone. Chris yells at his mother for packing Ann's bag, but she replies that everybody has to wait for Larry to come home. She is very insistent on this point. Chris says that he has let Larry go a long time ago. Mother cries that Larry is alive, because if he is dead, then Keller killed him. "As long as you live, that boy is alive. God does not let a son be killed by his father." She runs out.

Chris turns to Keller, finally understanding. Keller does not deny it; he ordered those cracked cylinder heads to be shipped out. Yet, they did not go into the type of plane that Larry flew. Chris says that Keller killed twenty-one men, and Chris then calls him a murderer. Keller explains that it was a matter of business: you work forty years, and in one moment, one failed shipment, the contracts can be torn up and you can lose everything. He thought that the military would notice the cracks anyway and that if they did not, he would warn them. But it was too late--the news was all over the papers that the planes had crashed, and the police were knocking on the door.

Chris is flabbergasted that his father suspected the planes would crash. Furious and betrayed, he asks why his father would do such a thing. For him, his father replies--for Chris, for the family, for the business. Enraged, Chris rants about his father's small-mindedness, in particular his lack of empathy with his countrymen and the human race. "No animal kills his own, what are you? What must I do to you?" He stumbles away, weeping, as his broken father cries out to him.

Analysis

Much of Miller's drama focuses on the unexceptional man. His Death of a Salesman is a fanfare for the common man, putting the dreary plights and small ambitions of the lower middle class into the anti-hero of Willy Loman. Miller finds high drama in the life of a man so common that he could be anyone in the audience, and that is why Death of a Salesman continues to resound so strongly with audiences, especially men of a certain age. Likewise, in The Crucible Miller takes commonplace people and puts them in the extraordinary situation of the Salem witch trials. The drama of the everyman is a trope throughout Miller's oeuvre, and it begins to surface as well in All My Sons, his first prominent play. The theme is first made apparent when Keller tries to justify Steve's actions during the war. He calls Steve a "little man," who buckled under pressure from the military when a shipment of cracked cylinder heads came through his inspection. Keller draws a distinction between men who are easily pressured and are natural followers (Steve) and men who can stand up for themselves and make the difficult choice in a bad situation (himself). The irony, of course, is that he is defending Steve a little too vehemently, because only he and his wife know that Keller actually belongs in the former category of the common follower. Keller may talk big, but we learn at the end of the second act that when the military was on the phone and he had to make a decision, Keller was the one who caved in to circumstance. The little man whom the hero patronizingly defends at the beginning of the play turns out to be rather like the hero himself.

Despite Keller's insistence that he was thinking of his family in the choice, it seems more likely that his first thought was on keeping his business. This emphasis, if true, reflects poorly not just on Keller but on the profit orientation of the capitalism within which he acts. Wartime racketeering and the merciless pursuit of business profit to the exclusion of human decency are, in Miller's worldview, part and parcel of the American capitalist system. Miller's leftist sympathies are no secret; the witch hunts of The Crucible are a thinly veiled allegory of the show trials of the McCarthy era, and Death of a Salesman is a virulent attack on a society that uses a man up during his working years and then leaves him out to dry when he is no longer useful. All My Sons was first produced before Miller's fame gave him the ability to launch more direct assaults on the ways that the profit-seeking elements of capitalism can tend to destroy American social structure, but the implicit critique is still salient here. Keller is not presented as a villain but as an ordinary man caught up in a bad situation and who makes a choice according to his own values. Indeed, if Keller really was thinking of his family, it would have been hard for him, in the Weberian, steel-hard shell of capitalist culture, to make a different choice. He might have lost the business and landed his family in poverty after all. Through Chris, nevertheless, Miller challenges Keller's individual or family values as misguided, ignorant, and destructive in relation to the larger social and cultural values he could have been paying attention to.

Even so, everyone intends to act in view of what one thinks is the good. Like Willy Loman, Keller is a tragic antihero, a relic from a simpler time before higher education and professionalization were widespread, when the nuclear family was truly the nucleus of a man's world and his community did not seem to extend to the whole world. Keller sees himself and his business as just one small cog in the American war machine, which is part of a world far beyond himself and his real influence. What he does not understand is that the actions of this small cog do have implications far wider than what he can see with his own eyes. He is answerable not to his family, but to his society. The issue is how to balance the competing claims of self, family, and society. Is it really acceptable to cause twenty-one people to die? His society thinks not, which is why Keller's associate was put in jail.

Moreover, Keller prefers to see himself as a victim of others. Instead of dealing with his complicity in a scandal that sent pilots to their deaths, Keller denies his involvement and passes off the blame, protecting his self-image and preserving the illusion that he has legitimately maintained his rightful place in society. When George opens up the old accusations, Keller is ready for him with a list of incidents in which George's father endangered the business. He is blind to the impulses within himself that make him just as dangerous as his meek and unassuming former partner, preferring to think of himself as a man among men, minding his own business (literally and figuratively). That is the true flaw in Keller's character; though he may not be fully faulted for imprecisely calibrating the complex values involved in his life, he denies the responsibility that he knows he should own up to. His denial, which keeps him out of jail, is paradoxically what ends up eating through his family's tranquility and locking him in his own self-imprisonment of shame and deception. And when the truth is finally revealed, at first through his wife's slip of the tongue, Keller tries to mitigate his guilt by portraying himself as the victim once more, dealing with forces outside his control.

Whereas before he belittled Steve for caving under the pressure, now he claims that the very same actions were the only sensible, businesslike things to do. He rationalizes that he was just serving the principles of good business, and that he thought the parts would hold up just fine in the air. But when Chris forces him to admit that he had his doubts about the planes' safety, he again justifies his decision by claiming that he was just one of thousands of men on the wartime profiteering bandwagon. "Who worked for nothin' in that war?" he asks. Yet his denials and deflections of blame, rather than assuaging his son, lead to Chris's complete disillusionment in the moral fiber of his father. (See Centola, 1997, on this topic.)

The dialogue in the second act varies between long, explanatory speeches, and fast exchanges characterized by extensive questioning. As the tension mounts, the questions grow shorter and more rapid-fire, increasing the pressure on Keller line by line. At the climax, the staccato dialogue heightens the drama of the courtroom-like confrontation between father and son. The stage directions indicate that "their movements now are those of subtle pursuit and escape." Where first Chris was asking questions about what happened and Keller was explaining, now Chris is hurling accusations and Keller is answering in defensive questions: "Dad, you killed twenty-one men!" "What, killed?" They are replaying the ancient dance of the archetypal father-son conflict. The act finishes with Chris's speech, building through eight questions, until he asks finally, "Don't you live in the world?" He then pulls back from that peak by redirecting the last question to himself, confessing that he does not know what to do. A son may find his father guilty, but how can he punish him? (See Griffin, 1996.)

Summary and Analysis of Act III

It is now the middle of the night. Mother is outside on a rocking chair, waiting for Chris to come home. Jim appears and asks about the fight. He knows the truth about Keller and Steve--he figured it out a long time ago. Mother says she thought that Chris sort of knew, as well, and she did not realize it would be such a shock to him. Jim says that Chris would never know how to live with a thing like that. But he will come back, because every man has to compromise his ideals sometime. Chris probably just wanted to be alone to watch "the star of his honesty" go out. Jim points out that he returned to his wife after having left her to do medical research, because he is a good husband; likewise, Chris will return because he is a good son. Jim leaves.

Keller enters. Mother tells him that when Chris returns, Keller will have to explain himself, making sure that Chris knows that Keller understands the gravity of his offense. That is, she wants Keller to offer to go to prison, should Chris ask him to. Keller does not like this plan, because he thinks he made the choice for the sake of his wife and son. Furthermore, he spoiled them rather than making them earn their keep. Mother says that these points do not excuse his crime. Keller insists that nothing is greater than the family, but there is something still greater in Chris's mind. Keller says starkly that Chris will forgive him, because "I'm his father and he's my son, and if there's something bigger than that I'll put a bullet in my head." Keller says that Larry would have understood; Larry had a head for business.

Ann enters and presents a plan to the Kellers. They have made Chris feel guilty for loving her, so she insists that Mother tell Chris that Larry is dead and she knows it, so that they can go away and be happy. "You had two sons. But you've only got one now," she says. But Mother refuses, because she knows in her heart that Larry is alive, and she knows that Chris and Ann must feel the same in their hearts. Ann says that she knows that Larry is dead. "Would I have looked at anyone else if I wasn't sure?" she asks rhetorically. Mother senses that there is something Ann is not saying.

Ann removes a letter from her pocket. It is a letter from Larry, which she never intended to show anyone unless it was necessary to allow her and Chris to get married. He wrote it right before he disappeared. As Mother reads the letter, she begins to moan, and Ann insists that the circumstances forced her to show the letter, since Mother would not believe Ann's word.

Chris returns and says that he will leave town because he cannot bear to be around his father with the knowledge he now has. He could jail him if he were human any more, but "I'm like everybody else now. You made me practical." Ann says she will go with him, but he says no, because in her heart she will always be asking him to send his father to jail. She says he should do what he has to do, but he cannot find a reason to make Keller suffer; after all, putting him behind bars will not raise the dead.

Keller returns and Chris walks away, saying that he has nothing to say to him. Keller asks what is bothering Chris--too much money? Then give it to charity. Chris can do what he wants with it; the money is his. Chris responds that the issue is what Keller wants to do. Keller rejoins that Chris cannot tell him to go to jail, because Keller clearly does not belong there. Besides, no one worked for free during the war. Wartime is profit time, and if he has to go to jail then half the country has to go with him. Chris understands but had thought Keller was better than the average, being his father. Chris feels unable to look at Keller or himself.

Ann gives Chris the letter, though Mother tries to stop him, or at least stop him from telling Keller what is in the letter. But Chris reads the letter aloud. Larry's letter is from the day he died. He had just seen the papers and heard about his father and the planes crashing. Larry felt full of guilt and anger, and wrote that he could not face anybody. He wrote that he was about to go out on a mission and that he would be reported missing. The letter implies suicide. Larry's letter to Ann adds that he loves her but that she must not wait for him.

Keller is quiet. He understands. He calls for the car and is ready to go upstairs to get a jacket. Mother tries to stop him, saying that Larry would not have sent him to jail. But Keller says that this is exactly what Larry is saying in the letter. "I think to him they were all my sons"--all the pilots who died. He goes upstairs. Mother turns to Chris and pleads with him not to take Keller to jail, but Chris says that nobody could stop Keller now. Mother says that the war is over--all these things are over--he cannot take away her husband. Chris responds that Keller should not just feel sorry; Larry died not just for that. She asks what more could be done, and Chris gives her a way to become better: "Once and for all you can know there's a universe of people outside and you're responsible to it, and unless you know that, you threw away your son because that's why he died."

A gunshot is heard in the house. Chris runs inside and tells Ann to find the doctor. Mother stays outside and moans her husband's name. Chris comes out in tears and says, "Mother, I didn't mean to-" But she interrupts him and tells him not to take the blame for his father's suicide. "Forget now. Live."

Analysis

Like her husband, Mother is in denial. She knows about Keller's guilt, and it is the source of her anxiety and headaches throughout the play. She is complicit in Keller's denial, and as for her own denial, she is forcing her son to stay alive, if only in her mind, in order to allow her to continue to live with her husband in some acceptable way. That is, if she had to accept that her husband effectively killed their son, then she could not bear it. But her loyalty to Keller ironically serves to separate the couple, since her knowledge of his guilt strains their relationship. Like her husband, she prefers to believe that there are forces outside her control--in her case, astrology and God's choice, both on Larry's side--that ultimately dictate life or death more than individual choice does.

But all this is not the blind trust of a grief-stricken mother. Just as she mistakenly thought that Chris always knew in the back of his mind that Keller was guilty, she always knew in her heart that Larry was dead, despite a play full of protestations to the contrary. When Ann shows her the letter that proves Larry's death, Mother suffers no great shock. Like Martha in Edward Albee's *Who's Afraid of Virginia Woolf*, she learns the "death" of a son who did not really exist anymore anyway. She knew--she always knew. What mattered was that no one said it aloud, because that way she would not have to examine the implications. And again like Albee's Martha, what truly died was not the son, but the mother's self-deception, the universe she had constructed inside her head in order to cope with the painful truth.

The title of the play becomes clear in Keller's final line. After years of denial, he is forced to acknowledge that the soldiers who died as a direct result of his actions were someone's sons, and they all might as well have been his sons. But this line, with the title, actually serves two independent arguments that run through the work. "All My Sons" has both an emotional center and an intellectual center. The emotional "All My Sons" has the Keller family at its core, being primarily concerned with the impact of shameful secrets on family relationships, in particular how their past can come back to haunt the present. When the work is performed, audiences are usually struck the hardest by the story of the crime and its consequences for the Keller family.

But the intellectual "All My Sons" is the story of that same crime and its consequences not for the Keller family, but for the world. If Miller is proposing a world-scale ethic of concern for everyone's sons, he proposes that Keller (and each member of the audience) should find in himself a kind of generalized care for all of the sons and daughters in the world. Miller later wrote that he wanted the play to be about "unrelatedness," describing Keller as a man who "cannot admit that he, personally, has any viable connection with his world, his universe, or his society." The admission that the pilots were "all my sons" is, for Keller, an admission that he might as well have killed his own child. The admission is also a new understanding that it should not matter whether the dead pilots could have been his sons; rather, we all have an obligation to society to value everyone's sons as though they were our own. Whether that level of concern is possible or feasible, indeed whether it is healthy and desirable to refuse to help your own children and neighbors while you try to help the whole world, is a different question, but the idealist might give it a try.

The tension among these values is highlighted throughout the play in Keller's and Chris's conflicting moralities. For Keller, there is nothing more important in this world than the family. For Chris, the destruction of the war wrought a new "kind of--responsibility. Man for man." And in the play, Keller's morality actually eclipses Chris's, even though Miller is giving the audience a shot at accepting Chris's leftist argument. In the end, what draws audiences is the emotion of a comprehensible, identifiable unit of society--that is, the drama of the nuclear family. The primacy of Miller's unrelatedness argument is defeated by its own truth. We will always care more about the one son whose father we see before us and with whom we identify, than the twenty-one dead sons who are not our own. At least, however, we can rise to the responsibility of making wise and prudent decisions to honor both the one and the twenty-one as well as we can.

Suggested Essay Questions

1. Several characters in the play believe in forces outside their control that influence the events of their lives. Kate turns to astronomy and God, while Keller argues that the pressures of business forced him to act as he did. Examine the role of personal agency in the play. For example, does Keller's suicide reflect a new acceptance of his misdeeds? Does he kill himself out of choice or mainly as a result of external pressures?
2. Keller argues that no one "worked for nothin' in that war," insisting that if he has to go to jail, then "half the Goddam country" is similarly culpable. Is this an indictment of capitalism or of the wartime mentality? Does he believe this argument, or is it mainly another attempt to deflect blame?
3. Did Kate (Mother) know that Larry was dead? Did Chris know that his father was guilty? How might the actors and director of the play keep these questions ambiguous or suggest that these facts were known all along? Did Miller possibly intend that the audience never know how much Kate and Chris had suspicions, or is the play better if the audience gradually learns that Kate and Chris knew the truth all along?
4. Which kinds of facts are better to face immediately, and which kinds are better to deny as long as possible? Consider personal, family, and social values. Use the play for possible anecdotal evidence.
5. The tone of much of the second and third acts is accusatory, with a strong emphasis on questions and questioning. How do the characters use questions to deflect blame? Or, how does Miller use questions to pace the dialogue and heighten the tension? What counts as evidence of the facts? (Consider the courtroom scenes in The Crucible for comparison.)
6. How does Miller introduce the past and show the effects of the past on the Kellers without employing flashbacks?
7. How does Miller manipulate information? The entirety of the first act is exposition, yet the audience is kept guessing and alert through Miller's careful pacing of the revelation of facts. How does our experience of the play change after we have seen it the first time and know all the history? Do successive iterations of reading or watching the play help us pick up on additional details of the themes and characters?
8. The common theatrical device of "the letter" provides a way for Larry to personally enter the play after his death. What else makes the letter work well in this particular play? Consider, for instance, Miller's careful manipulation of information throughout the play.
9. How does Miller characterize Larry, who never appears on stage but who is so fundamental to the events and the people? How can we reconcile or add together the various accounts of his character?
10. If the focus is on the Keller family, what is the point of including the Deever family as more than just a set of foils for the Kellers?

Influences on All My Sons

All My Sons is a tightly constructed household drama in the style of the ancient Greek tragedies and of the Norwegian playwright Henrik Ibsen. Ibsen was one of the forerunners of the modern realistic style of drama. In the second half of the nineteenth century, Ibsen's plays featured small casts, colloquial language, and realistic situtations. But from these realistic situations arose timeless, archetypal emotions and conflicts. Essentially, Ibsen took the high drama of the gods in Greek theater and set it anew in Victorian drawing rooms, with pistols and purses rather than lightning bolts and chariots.

In a time when the Norwegian theater was still full of morality plays, Ibsen's plays were highly controversial. Right and wrong were not immediately apparent, nor were there clear protagonists and antagonists. More shockingly, bad things often happened to good people, contrary to the poetic justice of most Victorian theater and of an audience's natural preferences.

Ibsen challenged such assumptions and conventions with, for example, powerful, complex female characters such as Hedda Gabler in A Doll's House), antiheroes such as in *Peer Gynt*, and critiques of mob mentality in plays such as *Enemy of the People*. His plays introduced idiomatic dialogue to the stage and a sense of realism that was adopted by Chekhov, Shaw, and realist playwrights through Miller. Ibsen is also credited with presenting scathing social critiques through the drama of individuals, taking the generalism of Greek tragedies (in which the heroes were often explicitly representative of all humanity or of particular human flaws) and compressing it into realistic individuals with whom, like Willy Loman, audiences could readily identify.

Ibsen's style and construction influenced all of Western theater, not just Arthur Miller's works. But Miller is particularly pinpointed as an Ibsenian playwright, even though his more fantastic works such as Death of a Salesman and *After the Fall* are very unlike Ibsen? Miller was an Ibsenian also because he wrote characters, like Joe Keller, Willy Loman, and John Proctor, who fit the Ibsenian mold of tragic Greek heroes in their contemporary world. All My Sons was particularly perceived as Ibsenian because of its structural and thematic similarities to Ibsen.

All My Sons owes a great debt to Ibsen's *The Wild Duck* (1884), in which a young man returns home and slowly discovers heinous secrets about his family. The protagonist insists on full truth in all statements, but his ideals end up backfiring and result in the suicide of a young girl, showing that some truths are too much to bear. This play bears thematic and structural similarities to All My Sons, which probably reinforced the critical reception of Miller as an Ibsenian playwright at the time.

The link of All My Sons to Greek tragedy is not just by way of Ibsen but more direct as well. The concept of the inescapable influence of the past is very classical (remember Oedipus, for example). Oedipus too discovers the full truth about killing his father and marrying his mother after a series of hints, and the past does determine the future. Likewise, the father-son conflict in which the son realizes that his father is a mere mortal and kills him (directly or indirectly) is one of the most classic tropes in drama.

All My Sons weaves together these elements--Greek themes, Ibsenian structure, and a modern idiom--into a triumph of the well-constructed realist play.

Author of ClassicNote and Sources

Elizabeth Weinbloom, author of ClassicNote. Completed on July 20, 2006, copyright held by GradeSaver.

Updated and revised Adam Kissel August 26, 2006. Copyright held by GradeSaver.

Gottfried, Martin. Arthur Miller; His Life and Work. Cambridge, MA: Da Capo Press, 2003.

Griffin, Alice. Understanding Arthur Miller. Columbia: University of South Carolina Press, 1996.

Miller, Arthur. All My Sons. New York: Nelson Doubleday, 1947.

Blumberg, Paul. "Work as Alienation in the Plays of Arthur Miller." *Arthur Miller: New Perspectives*. Ed. Robert A. Martin. Englewood Cliffs, NJ: Prentice-Hall, 1982.

Centola, Steven R. "*All My Sons*." *Cambridge Companion to Arthur Miller*. Ed. Christopher Bigsby. Cambridge: Cambridge University Press, 1997.

Moss, Leonard. "Colloquial Language in *All My Sons*." *Arthur Miller: New Perspectives*. Ed. Robert A. Martin. Englewood Cliffs, NJ: Prentice-Hall, 1982.

Quiz 1

1. **In what year was All My Sons first produced?**
   - A. 1945
   - B. 1947
   - C. 1949
   - D. 1951

2. **Who directed the first production of All My Sons?**
   - A. George Abbott
   - B. Elia Kazan
   - C. Joseph Papp
   - D. Eugene O'Neill

3. **What was Arthur Miller's first Broadway play?**
   - A. The View From the Bridge
   - B. All My Sons
   - C. The Man Who Had All the Luck
   - D. Death of a Salesman

4. **Which woman did Arthur Miller marry?**
   - A. Audrey Hepburn
   - B. Marilyn Monroe
   - C. Natalie Wood
   - D. Vivien Leigh

5. **What was Arthur Miller's religious background?**
   - A. Jewish
   - B. Baptist
   - C. Anglican
   - D. Catholic X Jewish

6. **How many performances did All My Sons run in its original production?**
   - A. 4
   - B. 328
   - C. 674
   - D. 1029

7. **Who "named names" for Senator McCarthy and HUAC?**

A. Arthur Miller, Elia Kazan, and Eugene O'Neill
B. Arthur Miller and Elia Kazan
C. Arthur Miller
D. Elia Kazan

8. **In what order were Miller's biggest plays produced?**

A. All My Sons, Death of a Salesman, The Crucible
B. Death of a Salesman, All My Sons, The Crucible
C. All My Sons, The Crucible, Death of a Salesman
D. Death of a Salesman, The Crucible, All My Sons

9. **What is Jim Bayliss's profession?**

A. Manufacturing
B. Medicine
C. Research
D. Law

10. **What does Jim Bayliss tell Ann not to do?**

A. Give her husband money
B. Hide her husband's money
C. Spend her husband's money
D. Count her husband's money

11. **What is in the basement of the Keller house, according to Bert?**

A. A fire station
B. A dungeon
C. A police station
D. A jail

12. **What does George Deever do for a living?**

A. Manufacturing
B. Medicine
C. Research
D. Law

13. **What does Jim Bayliss want to do with his life?**
   A. Medical research
   B. Patient advocacy
   C. Doctors Without Borders
   D. Charity work

14. **What was Lydia Lubey's relationship with George Deever?**
   A. They were classmates
   B. They were sweethearts
   C. They were rivals
   D. They were married

15. **Of what does Kate ask Frank Lubey to determine the probability?**
   A. If Larry disappeared on his "favorable day"
   B. If Larry disappeared on Kate's "favorable day"
   C. If Larry was born on his "favorable day"
   D. If Larry was born on Kate's "favorable day"

16. **In which month was Larry born?**
   A. August
   B. November
   C. July
   D. March

17. **In which month was Larry reported missing?**
   A. August
   B. November
   C. July
   D. March

18. **In which month does the play take place?**
   A. August
   B. November
   C. July
   D. March

19. **Where is the setting of the play?**
A. The Kellers' backyard
B. The Kellers' backyard and the manufacturing plant
C. The Kellers' backyard and the Bayliss's house
D. The Kellers' backyard and the Bayliss's backyard

20. **How did Larry's tree fall?**
A. Lightning struck it
B. Chris cut it down
C. Gardner cut it down
D. It fell because it was sick

21. **Before the start of the play, who knew about Larry's letter?**
A. Ann and Mother
B. Ann
C. Ann and Chris
D. Ann and George

22. **Where do George and Ann live?**
A. New York
B. Cleveland
C. Los Angeles
D. Washington

23. **How many P-40s crashed due to the parts from Keller's factory?**
A. 4
B. 21
C. 25
D. 36

24. **Who first saw that Larry's tree had fallen?**
A. Keller
B. Mother
C. Jim
D. Chris

25. **Which "sign" did NOT make Mother think Larry was returning?**

A. He disappeared on his favorable day

B. She stumbled over his baseball glove

C. Ann came home

D. His tree fell

Quiz 1 Answer Key

1. **(B)** 1947
2. **(B)** Elia Kazan
3. **(C)** The Man Who Had All the Luck
4. **(B)** Marilyn Monroe
5. **(A)** Jewish
6. **(B)** 328
7. **(D)** Elia Kazan
8. **(A)** All My Sons, Death of a Salesman, The Crucible
9. **(B)** Medicine
10. **(D)** Count her husband's money
11. **(D)** A jail
12. **(D)** Law
13. **(A)** Medical research
14. **(B)** They were sweethearts
15. **(A)** If Larry disappeared on his "favorable day"
16. **(A)** August
17. **(B)** November
18. **(A)** August
19. **(A)** The Kellers' backyard
20. **(A)** Lightning struck it
21. **(B)** Ann
22. **(A)** New York
23. **(B)** 21
24. **(B)** Mother
25. **(C)** Ann came home

Quiz 2

1. **Who said it? "Today a doctor could make a million dollars if he could figure out a way to bring a boy ino the world without a trigger finger."**
   A. Keller
   B. Mother
   C. Jim
   D. Chris

2. **"If I have to grub for money all day long at least at evening I want it beautiful."**
   A. Keller
   B. Ann
   C. Jim
   D. Chris

3. **"It's so funny ... everything decides to happen at the same time."**
   A. Keller
   B. Mother
   C. Ann
   D. Chris

4. **"What does that mean, me above all?"**
   A. Keller
   B. Mother
   C. Ann
   D. Chris

5. **"When you marry, never--even in your mind--never count your husband's money."**
   A. Jim
   B. Sue
   C. Frank
   D. Lydia

6. **"They don't say it on the radio but I'm sure that in the dark at night they're still waiting for their sons."**
   A. Mother
   B. Ann
   C. Sue
   D. Chris

7. **"But there's God, so certain things can never happen."**
   A. Keller
   B. Mother
   C. Ann
   D. Chris

8. **"The man was a fool, but don't make a murderer out of him."**
   A. Keller
   B. Mother
   C. Ann
   D. Chris

9. **"One new thing was made. A kind of--responsibility. Man for man."**
   A. George
   B. Ann
   C. Jim
   D. Chris

10. **"Be smart now. The boy is coming. Be smart."**
   A. Keller
   B. Mother
   C. Ann
   D. Chris

11. **"Men are like little boys, for the neighbors they'll always cut the grass."**
   A. Mother
   B. Ann
   C. Sue
   D. Lydia

12. **"You can never owe somebody without resenting them."**
   A. Mother
   B. Ann
   C. Sue
   D. Lydia

13. **"As soon as you get to know somebody you find a distinction for them."**
  A. Mother
  B. Ann
  C. Sue
  D. Chris

14. **"Everybody's gettin' so Goddam educated in this country there'll be nobody to take away the garbage."**
  A. George
  B. Keller
  C. Mother
  D. Chris

15. **"You stand on the street today and spit, you're gonna hit a college man."**
  A. George
  B. Keller
  C. Jim
  D. Frank

16. **"He's a little man. That's what happens to suckers, you know."**
  A. George
  B. Keller
  C. Jim
  D. Chris

17. **"Is it junk to feel that there's a greater power than ourselves?"**
  A. Mother
  B. Ann
  C. Frank
  D. Lydia

18. **"God does not let a son be killed by his father."**
  A. Keller
  B. Mother
  C. Ann
  D. Chris

19. **"What must I do, Jesus God, what must I do?"**
   A. Keller
   B. Mother
   C. Ann
   D. Chris

20. **"He probably just wanted to be alone to watch his star go out."**
   A. Mother
   B. Ann
   C. Jim
   D. Chris

21. **"It don't excuse it that you did it for the family."**
   A. George
   B. Mother
   C. Ann
   D. Chris

22. **"Would I have looked at anyone else if I wasn't sure?"**
   A. Mother
   B. Ann
   C. Lydia
   D. Chris

23. **"I'm like everybody else now. I'm practical now. You made me practical."**
   A. Keller
   B. Ann
   C. Jim
   D. Chris

24. **"Who worked for nothing in that war?"**
   A. George
   B. Keller
   C. Mother
   D. Chris

25. **Who is being spoken about? "He'd like to take every man who made money in the war and put him up against a wall."**
   A. George
   B. Keller
   C. Chris
   D. Steve

Quiz 2 Answer Key

1. **(A)** Keller
2. **(D)** Chris
3. **(B)** Mother
4. **(A)** Keller
5. **(A)** Jim
6. **(A)** Mother
7. **(B)** Mother
8. **(A)** Keller
9. **(D)** Chris
10. **(B)** Mother
11. **(C)** Sue
12. **(C)** Sue
13. **(B)** Ann
14. **(B)** Keller
15. **(B)** Keller
16. **(A)** George
17. **(C)** Frank
18. **(B)** Mother
19. **(D)** Chris
20. **(C)** Jim
21. **(B)** Mother
22. **(B)** Ann
23. **(D)** Chris
24. **(B)** Keller
25. **(D)** Steve

Quiz 3

1. **How did Larry die?**
    A. Suicide
    B. His plane was shot down
    C. Pneumonia
    D. His plane malfunctioned

2. **Why did Jim leave his wife?**
    A. To be free of her nagging for a while
    B. For a bettter job out of town
    C. To do research in New Orleans
    D. For another woman

3. **In what branch of the military did Larry serve?**
    A. Marines
    B. Air Force
    C. Army
    D. Navy

4. **What kind of juice does George like?**
    A. Orange
    B. Cranberry
    C. Grape
    D. Apple

5. **Approximately what year does All My Sons take place?**
    A. 1941
    B. 1944
    C. 1947
    D. 1951

6. **Why did Chris ask Ann to visit?**
    A. To see if he was still attracted to her
    B. To find out if she was still waiting for Larry
    C. To propose
    D. To ask her out

7. **Why did George visit his father in jail?**
   A. To hear his father's side of the story
   B. To tell him that Ann was getting married
   C. To ask forgiveness
   D. To yell at him

8. **Where is Steve's jail?**
   A. Richmond
   B. Portland
   C. Columbus
   D. Little Rock

9. **What did Mother dream?**
   A. That Larry was flying over the house in his plane
   B. That Larry had amnesia in a hospital in Switzerland
   C. That Larry was coming home the next day
   D. That Larry's tree woke up and danced a jig

10. **What is strange about Larry's room?**
   A. There are pictures of Ann on the wall
   B. Nothing has been touched and there is dust on everything
   C. All the shoes are shined and the clothes are pressed
   D. It was made into a home gym

11. **What room does Ann stay in?**
   A. Chris's
   B. Larry's
   C. Mother's
   D. The living room

12. **Which is NOT a reason why Mother thinks Larry is alive?**
   A. He disappeared on his favorable day
   B. God would not let that happen
   C. His plane was found with no body in it
   D. She would know in her heart if he was dead

13. **Why isn't Keller in jail?**
   A. He was let out on parole
   B. He won his appeal
   C. He escaped
   D. He wasn't convicted

14. **What does Frank do for a living?**
   A. Haberdashery
   B. Manufacturing
   C. Fortune telling
   D. Astrology

15. **Do people still talk about the case?**
   A. No, it's old news
   B. No, everyone believes Keller was innocent
   C. Yes, and they shun the Kellers
   D. Yes, though they are still nice to the Kellers

16. **What did Keller do the day he got out of jail?**
   A. Wrote a letter to the editor of the local newspaper
   B. Walked down the block in broad daylight
   C. Had a really nice sandwich
   D. Opened his factory for business

17. **What kind of planes crashed?**
   A. F-20
   B. F-40
   C. P-20
   D. P-40

18. **What does Keller offer Steve?**
   A. A place to stay
   B. Partnership in the business
   C. A kick in the teeth
   D. A job when he gets out

19. **At the start of the play, what is Chris's relationship with his parents?**
    A. Polite but distanced
    B. Bitter and resentful
    C. Variable
    D. Very loving

20. **How did Chris kiss Ann?**
    A. Like a cold fish
    B. Like a ladies' man
    C. Like Larry
    D. Like Larry's brother

21. **How many of Chris's men survived the war?**
    A. All of them
    B. Half of them
    C. A few of them
    D. None of them

22. **What brought about Chris's idealism?**
    A. A near-death experience
    B. A religious conversion
    C. The destruction he saw in the war
    D. Larry's death

23. **Why is Mother nervous about George's visit?**
    A. She thinks he wants to borrow money
    B. She thinks he wants to reopen the case
    C. She thinks he is a pain in the neck
    D. She thinks he wants to break up the engagement

24. **Why do Chris and Ann keep Mother in the dark about their engagement?**
    A. She thinks Ann is not good enough for Chris
    B. She thinks Chris is not good enough for Ann
    C. She thinks Chris cannot afford a family yet
    D. She thinks Larry is alive

25. **Who picked up George at the train?**

A. Keller

B. Ann

C. Jim

D. Chris

Quiz 3 Answer Key

1. **(A)** Suicide
2. **(C)** To do research in New Orleans
3. **(B)** Air Force
4. **(C)** Grape
5. **(C)** 1947
6. **(C)** To propose
7. **(B)** To tell him that Ann was getting married
8. **(C)** Columbus
9. **(A)** That Larry was flying over the house in his plane
10. **(C)** All the shoes are shined and the clothes are pressed
11. **(B)** Larry's
12. **(C)** His plane was found with no body in it
13. **(B)** He won his appeal
14. **(A)** Haberdashery
15. **(D)** Yes, though they are still nice to the Kellers
16. **(B)** Walked down the block in broad daylight
17. **(D)** P-40
18. **(D)** A job when he gets out
19. **(D)** Very loving
20. **(D)** Like Larry's brother
21. **(D)** None of them
22. **(C)** The destruction he saw in the war
23. **(B)** She thinks he wants to reopen the case
24. **(D)** She thinks Larry is alive
25. **(C)** Jim

Quiz 4

1. **Why does Sue dislike Chris?**
    A. He flirts with all the girls
    B. He lives off his parents
    C. He told her husband to leave her
    D. He makes her husband feel guilty

2. **What does Sue ask Ann to do?**
    A. Not marry Chris
    B. Tell Chris to stop pushing his idealism on Jim
    C. Make Chris give money to charity
    D. Move away with Chris to a different town

3. **In whose house do the Baylisses live?**
    A. Larry's
    B. Ann's and George's
    C. The Lubeys'
    D. The Kellers' backyard and the Bayliss's backyard

4. **What does Sue do for a living?**
    A. Receptionist
    B. Nursing
    C. Research
    D. House wife

5. **Where did Keller go to college?**
    A. Rhodes College
    B. The state university
    C. Back east
    D. Night school

6. **To whom is there nothing greater than family?**
    A. Keller
    B. Keller and Chris
    C. Keller and Mother
    D. Chris

7. **Whose hat does George wear?**
   A. Chris's
   B. His own
   C. Keller's
   D. His father's

8. **What did Keller tell Steve to do with the defective shipment?**
   A. Send it out as is
   B. Weld the cracks and send it out
   C. Send it out with a note explaining the defect
   D. Reseal the boxes and send them out

9. **Why was it that George used to believe Keller's story?**
   A. He loved Keller
   B. He did not know the whole story
   C. Chris believed it
   D. He did not trust his father

10. **What leads George to determine what really happened?**
   A. Jim says Keller is the healthiest man he ever saw
   B. Mother says Keller has not been laid up in fifteen years
   C. Mother says Keller never had the flu
   D. Steve says Keller was not actually sick

11. **How does Mother treat George when he arrives?**
   A. She tells him to get married
   B. She ignores him
   C. She is polite to him
   D. She feeds him

12. **With whom does Mother try to set George up?**
   A. Ann
   B. Mr. Marcy's daughter
   C. Lydia
   D. The neighbor

13. **What does Keller's factory make now?**
   A. Airplane parts
   B. A little of everything
   C. Cars
   D. Nothing, it's closed

14. **How does Chris find out the truth about Keller?**
   A. George tells him
   B. Keller tells him
   C. Mother tells him
   D. Mother says that Keller has been healthy for fifteen years

15. **What excuse does Keller NOT use for why he sent out the defective parts?**
   A. He was going to tell them about the defects before it was too late.
   B. He thought the defect would never affect the safety of the planes
   C. He felt threatened that the army would tear up his contract
   D. He thought the military would catch the defect

16. **How did Jim find out the truth?**
   A. Chris told him
   B. Mother told him
   C. He saw Keller out of bed when he was supposedly sick
   D. He guessed a long time ago

17. **Where does Mother ask Keller to go, should Chris ask him to?**
   A. To jail
   B. To visit Steve
   C. To court
   D. To church

18. **When did Larry write his last letter?**
   A. Right before he shot himself
   B. Right after he wrote to Chris
   C. Right after he found out about the scandal at home
   D. Right before he went out on his last mission

19. **Who reads the letter aloud?**
    A. Keller
    B. Mother
    C. Ann
    D. Chris

20. **Will Chris send Keller to jail?**
    A. No; he is practical now
    B. No; he is scared for his safety
    C. Yes; Keller is clearly guilty
    D. No; the evidence is not strong enough

21. **What does Ann ask Chris to do toward the end?**
    A. Do not send his father to jail
    B. Send his father to jail
    C. Set her father free
    D. Whatever he wants to do about his father

22. **Whose money is it?**
    A. Chris's
    B. Keller's
    C. The whole family's
    D. Ann's

23. **Why did Chris expect more from Keller?**
    A. Keller was his father
    B. Keller was incapable of such a crime
    C. Keller respected the military
    D. Keller was a good man

24. **What does Keller suggest he will do at the end?**
    A. Run away
    B. Go to jail
    C. Free Steve
    D. Kill himself

25. **What does Keller actually do in the end?**

A. Run away
B. Go to jail
C. Free Steve
D. Kill himself

Quiz 4 Answer Key

1. **(D)** He makes her husband feel guilty
2. **(D)** Move away with Chris to a different town
3. **(B)** Ann's and George's
4. **(B)** Nursing
5. **(D)** Night school
6. **(A)** Keller
7. **(D)** His father's
8. **(B)** Weld the cracks and send it out
9. **(C)** Chris believed it
10. **(B)** Mother says Keller has not been laid up in fifteen years
11. **(D)** She feeds him
12. **(B)** Mr. Marcy's daughter
13. **(B)** A little of everything
14. **(C)** Mother tells him
15. **(B)** He thought the defect would never affect the safety of the planes
16. **(D)** He guessed a long time ago
17. **(A)** To jail
18. **(D)** Right before he went out on his last mission
19. **(D)** Chris
20. **(A)** No; he is practical now
21. **(D)** Whatever he wants to do about his father
22. **(A)** Chris's
23. **(A)** Keller was his father
24. **(B)** Go to jail
25. **(D)** Kill himself

19891126R00047

Printed in Great Britain
by Amazon